GOTCHA!

written by
GAIL JORGENSEN

illustrated by
KERRY ARGENT

SCHOLASTIC INC.
New York Toronto London Auckland Sydney

For Kris, Anita, and Janelle
— G. J.

ISBN 0-590-96209-4

 Published by Scholastic Inc., 555 Broadway, New York, NY 10012, by arrangement with Omnibus Books.

12 11 10 9 8 7 6 5 4 3 2 1 7 8 9/9 0 1 2/0

Printed in the U.S.A. 08

First Scholastic printing, November 1997

Right in the middle of Bertha Bear's party,

just as she was about to cut the cake...

a big, BLACK, beastly fly

buzzed in her ear,

flew up her nose,

walked on her pie,

AND...

dive-bombed her seven-layer birthday cake.

"GOTCHA!" cried Bertha.

Bzzzzz! went the fly.
"MISSED!"
growled Bertha.

Off went the fly,
and *off* went Bertha
to catch that
big, black, BEASTLY fly.

On and on they went...

over tufts of grass and lumpy mounds.

SWAT!
GOTCHA!

MISSED!

SWAT!
GOTCHA!

MISSED!

On and on they went...

over muddy banks and wobbly logs.

CRACK! GOTCHA!

MISSED!

WHACK!
GOTCHA!

MISSED!

On and on they went...

over pebbly paths and BIG round rocks.

WALLOP! GOTCHA!

MISSED!

On and on *and on* they went...

right back

to where they started from.

Humph! snorted the camel.
Grrr! snarled the crocodile.
Caw! cried the stork.
Ooof! grunted the tortoise.

"*Cake?*" asked Bertha.

Bzzzzz! went the fly.